PRINCIPLES OF ACCOUNTING

WORKING PAPERS 2A FOR EXERCISES AND A PROBLEMS, CHAPTERS 14–28

FOURTH EDITION

NOTE TO STUDENTS

This book contains Working Papers to be used in preparing solutions to all Exercises, A Problems and Comprehensive Problems for Chapters 14–28 and the Appendices in Principles of Accounting, Fourth Edition. The Working Papers are designed to simplify your work; appropriate forms for each exercise and problem are provided, and some preliminary information has been printed to help you get started.

Exercise 14-1 Partnership Formation

		General Journal			
Date		Description	Post. Ref.	Debit	Credit

Exercise 14-2 Distribution of Income and Losses and Computations

		General Journal			
Date		Description	Post. Ref.	Debit	Credit
1.					

Computations:

Exercise 14-2 (continued)

		General Journal			
Date		Description	Post. Ref.	Debit	Credit
2.					

Computations:

		General Journal			
Date		Description	Post. Ref.	Debit	Credit
3.					

Computations:

Exercise 14-2 (concluded)

	General Journal							
Date	Description	Post. Ref.		Debit			Credit	
4.								

		Davis	Johnson	Total

Exercise 14-3 Distribution of Income: Salary and Interest

		General Journal			
Date		Description	Post. Ref.	Debit	Credit
1.					

Computation:	Davis	Johnson	Total

Exercise 14-3 (continued)

		General Journal																			
Date		Description	Post. Ref.			Debit							Credit						
2.																			

Computation:	Davis	Johnson	Total

Exercise 14-3 (continued)

			General Journal																			
							Post.																
Date			Description				Ref.			Debit						Credit						
3.																						

Computation:		Davis		Johnson		Total	

Exercise 14-3 (concluded)

	General Journal			
Date	Description	Post. Ref.	Debit	Credit
4.				

Computation:		Davis	Johnson	Total

Exercise 14-4 Distribution of Income: Average Capital Balance

Average capital balance computed

Partner	Date	Capital Balance × Months Unchanged = Total			Average Capital

Average capital balance ratios computed

Distribution of income computed

Exercise 14-5 Admission of New Partner: Bonus to Old Partners

Date	Description	Post. Ref.	Debit	Credit
General Journal				
1.				

Computation:

Exercise 14-5 (continued)

		General Journal				
Date		Description	Post. Ref.	Debit		Credit
2.						

Computation:

Exercise 14-6 Withdrawal of Partner

			Post.		
Date	Description		Ref.	Debit	Credit

General Journal

Computation:

Exercise 14-7 Partnership Liquidation

1 Cash distribution to partners calculated

Description	Cash	Noncash Assets	=	Liabilities	+	Toney Capital	+	Cheeks Capital	+	Gain or (Loss) from Realization

Exercise 14-7 (continued)

2 *Journal entries prepared*

	General Journal				
Date	Description	Post. Ref.	Debit	Credit

Exercise 14-8 Partnership Liquidation

1 Cash distribution to partners calculated

Description	Cash	Assets	=	Liabilities	+	Barbara Capital	+	Ruth Capital	+	Meg Capital	+	Gain or (Loss) from Realization

1 *Disclosure of information on lawsuits*

2 *Effect of payment on clinic's financial statement and on doctors' financial situations*

1 Journal entry prepared

	General Journal				
Date	Description	Post. Ref.	Debit		Credit

2 *Share for each partner determined*

	19x1	19x2
a. Income and losses shared equally		
b. Income and losses shared in ratio 7:3		
c. Income shared in ratio of original investments		
d. Income and losses shared in ratio of beginning capital balances		

2 *(continued)*

	Chan	Nichols	Loss Distribution
e. Interest on investment; remainder equally			
19x1 Computation:			

	Chan	Nichols	Income Distribution
19x2 Computation:			

2 (concluded)

	Chan	Nichols	Loss Distribution
f. Interest and salaries allowed; remainder equally			
19x1 Computation:			

	Chan	Nichols	Income Distribution
19x2 Computation:			

1 *Income distribution calculated for $272,600 income*

	Gregory	Jerome	Owen	Income Distributed

2 *Income distribution calculated for $77,800 income*

	Gregory	Jerome	Owen	Income Distributed

3 *Income distribution calculated for $28,400 loss*

	Gregory	Jerome	Owen	Income Distributed

a, b, c, Journal entries prepared

		General Journal				
Date		Description	Post. Ref.		Debit	Credit

Computations:

d Journal entries prepared

	General Journal			
Date	Description	Post. Ref.	Debit	Credit

Computations:

e, f Journal entries prepared

Date	Description	Post. Ref.	Debit	Credit

General Journal

Computations:

Date	Description	Post. Ref.	Debit	Credit

General Journal

Problem 14A-4
Partnership Liquidation

1 Statement of liquidation prepared

Statement of Liquidation

Explanation	Cash	Accounts Receivable	Inventory	Equipment	Accounts Payable	Gary, Capital (50%)	Dawn, Capital (30%)	Leslie, Capital (20%)	Gain or (Loss) from Realization
Balance 7/31/xx	$6,000	$120,000	$264,000	$462,000	$480,000	$72,000	$180,000	$120,000	

2 *Journal entries prepared to record liquidation*

		General Journal			
Date		Description	Post. Ref.	Debit	Credit

Problem 14A-5
Comprehensive Partnership Transactions

	General Journal			
Date	Description	Post. Ref.	Debit	Credit
19x1				

Calculation:

	Flippo	McCovey	Loss Distributed

Comprehensive Partnership Transactions

	General Journal			
Date	Description	Post. Ref.	Debit	Credit
19x2				
Jan 1				

Calculation:

General Journal

Date		Description	Post. Ref.	Debit	Credit
19x2					
Dec	31				

Calculation:

	Flippo	McCovey	Sanford	Income Distributed

		General Journal				
Date		Description	Post. Ref.	Debit		Credit
19x3						

Flippo, McCovey, and Sanford Partnership
Statement of Liquidation
January 1, 19x3

Explanation	Cash	Accounts Receivable	Land	Building (Net)	Office Equipment (Net)	Accounts Payable	Mortgage Payable	Flippo, Capital (33.3%)	McCovey, Capital (33.3%)	Sanford, Capital (33.3%)	Gain or (Loss) from Realization
Balance 1/1/x3	$244,000	$152,000	$36,000	$280,000	$108,000	$108,000	$204,000	$168,960	$211,040	$128,000	

1 *Capital balance computed*

2 *Expected income analyzed for five years*

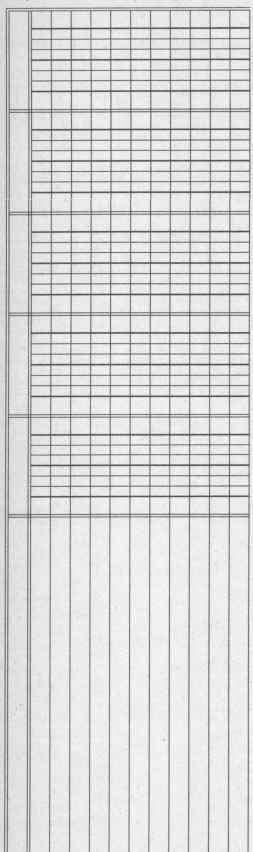

3 Counter offer developed

Exercise 15-1 Journal Entries for Organization Costs

			General Journal			
Date		Description	Post. Ref.	Debit		Credit

Exercise 15-2 Journal Entries and Stockholders' Equity

1 Journal entries prepared

	General Journal			
Date	Description	Post. Ref.	Debit	Credit

2 Stockholders' equity section prepared

Winkler Hospital Supply Corporation		
Stockholders' Equity		
March 1, 19xx		

Exercise 15-3 Stockholders' Equity

Aguilar Corporation		
Stockholders' Equity		
December 31, 19xx		

Exercise 15-4 Cash Dividends

		General Journal			
Date		Description	Post. Ref.	Debit	Credit

Exercise 15-5 Preferred Stock Dividends With Dividends in Arrears

	Preferred Stock Dividends		Common Stock Dividends		Total Dividends
	Amount	Per Share	Amount	Per Share	Allocated

Exercise 15-11 Exercise of Stock Options

		General Journal			
Date	Description	Post. Ref.	Debit	Credit

1 Stock issuance recorded

	General Journal				
Date	Description	Post. Ref.	Debit		Credit

2 Stockholders' equity prepared and discussed

UAL, Inc.		
Stockholders' Equity		
February 18, 1986 (in thousands)		

Discussion

3 Underwriter fee discussed

1 Journal entries prepared

		General Journal			
Date		Description	Post. Ref.	Debit	Credit

1 (continued)

		General Journal																					
Date		Description		Post. Ref.			Debit								Credit					

1 (concluded)

	General Journal			
Date	Description	Post. Ref.	Debit	Credit

2 *Stockholders' equity section of balance sheet prepared*

Abelman Corporation		
Stockholders' Equity		
December 31, 19xx		

1 Schedule of alternatives prepared

	Alternatives		
Northeast Servotech Corporation			
Schedule of Financial Alternatives			
19xx			
	A	B	C

2 *Cash requirements for first year computed*

3 The alternatives evaluated

Exercise 16-1 Statement of Retained Earnings

Snadhu Corporation							
Statement of Retained Earnings							
For the Year Ended December 31, 19x2							

Exercise 16-2 Journal Entries: Stock Dividends

General Journal					
Date	Description	Post. Ref.	Debit		Credit

Exercise 16-3 Stock Split

Before stock split			
After stock split			

		General Journal	Post.		
Date		Description	Ref.	Debit	Credit

Exercise 16-4 Treasury Stock Transactions

General Journal					
Date	Description	Post. Ref.	Debit	Credit	

Exercise 16-9 Use of Corporate Income Tax Rate Schedule

Situation A

Situation B

Situation C

Exercise 16-10 Income Tax Allocation

1 Amount of taxes paid computed

	19x2	19x3

2 Journal entries prepared

		General Journal			
Date		Description	Post. Ref.	Debit	Credit

Exercise 16-12 Corporate Income Statement

1 Income statement prepared

Dasbol Corporation								
Income Statement								
For the Year Ended December 31, 19x3								

Exercise 16-12 (continued)

2 Restructuring plan assessed

1 Partial income statement prepared

Lockheed Corporation		
Partial Income Statement		
For the Year Ended December 31, 1981		
(in millions of dollars)		

2 Stock market reaction discussed

Problem 16A-4
Corporate Income Statement

Daniels Shoe Corporation															
Income Statement															
For the Year Ended December 31, 19xx															

2 Statement of retained earnings prepared

Skolnick Company																	
Statement of Retained Earnings																	
For the Year Ended December 31, 19x2																	

3 Stockholders' equity section of balance sheet prepared

Skolnick Company		
Stockholders' Equity		
December 31, 19x2		

4 Book value per share computed

December 31, 19x1

December 31, 19x2

Financial Decision Case
Metzger Steel Corporation

1 T accounts and stockholders' equity section prepared (dollars in thousands)

Common Stock	Common Stock Distributable	Paid-in Capital in Excess of Par Value, Common

Retained Earnings	Treasury Stock, Common	Common Stock Outstanding (in thousands of shares)

Metzger Steel Corporation
Stockholders' Equity
December 31, 19xx
(in thousands of dollars)

2 *Arnold Metzger's position analyzed and discussed*

1 General journal entries prepared

		General Journal			
Date	Description	Post. Ref.	Debit		Credit
Jan 1	Cash		500000		
	Common Stock				100000
	Paid in Capital in excess				400000
	of par stated v, Common				
Jan 2	Organization Cost		60000		
	C Stock.				12000
	Paid in C in ex of S.V, C.				48000
Jan 3	Cash.		100000		
	Preferred Stock				100000
Feb 6	Subscriptions Rec.		360000		
	Common St Sub.				60000
	Paid in C. in ex of SV, C				300000
Mar 7	Patent A/c.		50000		
	C. Stock.				8000
	Paid in C in ex of SV, C.				42000
Apr 2	Cash		180000		
	Subs. Rec.				180000
	Common Stock Sub		180000		
	Common Stock				180000
May 5	Treasury Stock		240000		
	Cash				240000
May 19	Cash		117000		
	Treasury Stock				104000
	Paid in Capital, T.S				13000

1 (continued)

		General Journal				
Date		Description	Post. Ref.	Debit		Credit
June 30		Income Summary		250000		
		Retained Earnings				250000
July 8		Cash		49000		
		Paid in Capital, T.S.		7000		
		Treasury Stock				56000
Aug 4		Retained Earnings		100800		
		Common Stock Dist				12600
		Paid in C in ex of SV				88200
		C. S Dist		12600		
		C. S.				12600
Oct 10		Treasury St		90000		
		Cash				90000
		C. Stock		10000		
		Paid in		50000		
				30000		

1 *(continued)*

		General Journal				
Date		Description	Post. Ref.	Debit		Credit

1 (continued)

	General Journal			
Date	Description	Post. Ref.	Debit	Credit

2 *Statement of retained earnings prepared*

Sundial Corporation				
Statement of Retained Earnings				
For the Year Ended December 31, 19xx				

3 *Stockholders' equity section prepared*

Sundial Corporation			
Stockholders' Equity			
December 31, 19xx			

3 Supporting calculations for stockholders' equity section of balance sheet

3 (continued)

4 Book values for preferred and common stock computed

Exercise 17-1 Journal Entries for Interest Using the Straight-line Method

		General Journal			
Date		Description	Post. Ref.	Debit	Credit

Exercise 17-2 Journal Entries for Interest Using the Straight-line Method

	General Journal				
Date	Description	Post. Ref.	Debit		Credit

Exercise 17-3 Journal Entries for Interest Using the Effective Interest Method

		General Journal			
Date		Description	Post. Ref.	Debit	Credit

Exercise 17-4 Journal Entries for Interest Using the Effective Interest Method

		Post.		
Date	Description	Ref.	Debit	Credit

Exercise 17-5 Journal Entries for Interest Payments Using the Effective Interest Method

		General Journal			
Date		Description	Post. Ref.	Debit	Credit

Exercise 17-6 Valuing Bonds Using Present Value

Bond (a)		
Bond (b)		

Exercise 17-7 Zero Coupon Bonds

a.

b.

c.

d.

e.

Exercise 17-8 Zero Coupon Bonds

Face value of 30-year, 10% zero coupon bonds, compounded annually:

Face value of 50-year, 10% zero coupon bonds, compounded annually:

Face value of 30-year, 8% zero coupon bonds, compounded annually:

Face value of 50-year, 8% zero coupon bonds, compounded annually:

Exercise 17-9 Time Value of Money and Early Extinguishment of Debt

1 Current market value of the bond calculated

2 Retirement of bonds recorded

	General Journal			
Date	Description	Post. Ref.	Debit	Credit

Exercise 17-10 Bond Issue Entries

General Journal				
Date	Description	Post. Ref.	Debit	Credit

Exercise 17-11 Sales of Bonds between Interest Dates

1 Sale of bonds and first semiannual interest payment recorded

General Journal				
Date	Description	Post. Ref.	Debit	Credit

Exercise 17-11 (continued)

2 Amount of bond interest expense determined

Exercise 17-12 Year-end Accrual of Bond Interest

		General Journal			
Date	Description	Post. Ref.	Debit	Credit

Exercise 17-13 Bond Retirement Journal Entry

			General Journal			
Date		Description	Post. Ref.	Debit		Credit

Exercise 17-14 Bond Conversion Journal Entry

			General Journal			
Date		Description	Post. Ref.	Debit		Credit

Exercise 17-15 Mortgage Payable

1 Monthly payment schedule prepared

Month	Monthly Payment	Interest for One Month at 12% on Unpaid Balance	Reductions in Debt	Unpaid Balance at End of Period

2 Journal entries prepared

		General Journal			
Date		Description	Post. Ref.	Debit	Credit

Exercise 17-16 Recording Lease Obligations

1 Present value calculated

2 Lease agreement recorded

3 Depreciation for first year recorded

4 Lease payment recorded

		General Journal			
Date	Description	Post. Ref.	Debit	Credit

1 *Original issues recorded*

		General Journal				
Date		Description	Post. Ref.	Debit	Credit	

2 *Effective interest compounded*

3 *Bond interest expense recorded and discussed*

General Journal

Date	Description	Post. Ref.	Debit	Credit

Problem 17A-1
Bond Transactions — Straight-Line Method.

1 *Journal entries prepared for bonds issued at greater than face value*

2 *Journal entries prepared for bonds issued at less than face value*

Date	Description	Post. Ref.	Debit	Credit

3 Journal entries prepared for bonds issued at face value

	General Journal			
Date	Description	Post. Ref.	Debit	Credit

Problem 17A-2

Bond Transactions—Effective Interest Method

1 *Journal entries prepared for bonds issued at more than face value*

2 *Journal entries prepared for bonds issued at less than face value*

		General Journal			
Date		Description	Post. Ref.	Debit	Credit

3 *Journal entries prepared for bonds issued at face value*

	Date	Description	Post. Ref.	Debit	Credit

General Journal

Problem 17A-3
Bonds Issued at Discount and Premium

		General Journal			
Date		Description	Post. Ref.	Debit	Credit

		General Journal			
Date		Description	Post. Ref.	Debit	Credit

Name _____

1 Mortgage payment schedule prepared

Payment Date	Unpaid Balance at Beginning of Period	Monthly Payment	Interest for One Month at 1% on Unpaid Balance	Reduction in Debt	Unpaid Balance at End of Period

2 Journal entries prepared

	General Journal			
Date	Description	Post. Ref.	Debit	Credit

2 (concluded)

		General Journal				
Date		Description	Post. Ref.	Debit		Credit

1 *Interest and amortization table prepared*

Semiannual Interest Period	Carrying Value at Beginning of Period	Semiannual Interest Expense at $5\frac{1}{2}\%$ to Be Recorded	Semiannual Interest to Be Paid at $5\frac{8}{10}\%$ to Bondholders	Amortization of Premium	Unamortized Bond Premium at End of Period	Carrying Value at End of Period
0						
1						
2						
3						
4						
5						
6						
7						
8						
9						
10						

2 Journal entries prepared

	General Journal			
Date	Description	Post. Ref.	Debit	Credit

	Date		Description	Post. Ref.	Debit	Credit
General Journal						

		General Journal			
Date		Description	Post. Ref.	Debit	Credit

	General Journal			
Date	Description	Post. Ref.	Debit	Credit

1 Purchase using bonds payable entries prepared

		General Journal			
Date	Description	Post. Ref.	Debit	Credit

1 (continued)

Effects

2 *Capital lease entries recorded*

		General Journal			
Date		Description	Post. Ref.	Debit	Credit

2 (concluded)

Effects

3 Decision factors discussed

Exercise 18-1 Classification of Cash Flow Transactions

Transaction	Operating Activity	Investing Activity	Financing Activity	Non Cash Transaction	None
a. Declared and paid cash dividend					
b. Purchased an investment					
c. Received cash from customers					
d. Paid interest					
e. Sold equipment at a loss					
f. Issued long-term bonds for plant assets					
g. Received dividends on securities held					
h. Issued common stock					
i. Declared and issued a stock dividend					
j. Repaid notes payable					
k. Paid employees for wages					
l. Purchased a 60-day treasury bill					
m. Purchased land					

Exercise 18-2 Computing Cash Flows from Operating Activities — Direct Method

a. Cash receipts from sales

b. Cash payments for purchases

c. Cash payments for operating expenses

d. Cash payments for income taxes

Exercise 18-3 Computing Cash Flows from Operating Activities — Indirect Method

Mayfair Corporation					
Schedule of Cash Flows from Operating Activities					
For the Year Ended December 31, 19x1					

Exercise 18-4 Preparing a Schedule of Cash Flows from Operating Activities — Direct Method

Ridge Corporation					
Schedule of Cash Flows from Operating Activities					
For the Year Ended June 30, 19xx					

Exercise 18-4 (concluded)

Computations

(a)

(b)

(c)

(d)

Exercise 18-5 Preparing a Schedule of Cash Flows from Operating Activities — Indirect Method

Ridge Corporation												
Schedule of Cash Flows from Operating Activities												
For the Year Ended June 30, 19xx												

Exercise 18-6 Computing Cash Flows from Investing Activities — Investments

Exercise 18-10 Preparing a Worksheet for the Statement of Cash Flows

	Javier Corporation				
	Work Sheet for Statement of Cash Flows				
	For the Year Ended June 30, 19x2				
	Account Balances	Analysis of Transactions			Account Balances
Description	19x1	Debit		Credit	19x2
Debits					
Credits					
Cash Flows from Operating Activities					
Cash Flows from Investing Activities					
Cash Flows from Financing Activities					

Exercise 18-10 (concluded)

Javier Corporation																			
Statement of Cash Flows																			
For the Year Ended June 30, 19x2																			

1 Role of depreciation discussed

2 Net cash flows discussed

3 *Expansion discussed*

Transaction	Cash Flow Classification				Effect on Cash		
	Operating Activity	Investing Activity	Financing Activity	Noncash Transactions	Increase	Decrease	No Effect
a. Incurred net loss							
b. Declared/issued stock dividend							
c. Paid cash dividend							
d. Collected accounts receivable							
e. Purchased inventory with cash							
f. Retired long-term debt with cash							
g. Sold investment for a loss							
h. Issued stock for equipment							
i. Purchased insurance—cash							
j. Purchased treasury stock—cash							
k. Retired fully depreciated truck							
l. Paid interest on note							
m. Received dividend on investment							
n. Sold treasury stock							
o. Paid income taxes							
p. Transferred cash to money market account							
q. Purchased land and building with mortgage							

1 Schedule prepared—direct method

Milos Food Corporation		
Schedule of Cash Flows from Operating Activities		
For the Year Ended December 31, 19xx		

1 (concluded)

Computations

a.

b.

c.

d.

2 Schedule prepared—indirect method

Milos Food Corporation																		
Schedule of Cash Flows from Operating Activities																		
For the Year Ended December 31, 19xx																		

1 Schedule prepared—direct method

Gardner Electronics, Inc.		
Schedule of Cash Flows from Operating Activities		
For the Year Ended February 28, 19x3		

1 (continued)

Computations

a.

b.

c.

d.

2 *Schedule prepared—indirect method*

Gardner Electronics, Inc.		
Schedule of Cash Flows from Operating Activities		
For the Year Ended February 28, 19x3		

1 Worksheet prepared

	Meridian Corporation				
	Work Sheet for Statement of Cash Flows				
	For the Year Ended December 31, 19x2				
Description	Account Balances 12/31/x1	Analysis of Transactions Debit	Analysis of Transactions Credit	Account Balances 12/31/x2	
Debits					
Credits					
Cash Flows from Operating Activities					

1 (concluded)

	Account Balances 12/31/x1	Analysis of Transactions Debit	Analysis of Transactions Credit	Account Balances 12/31/x2
Cash Flows from Investing Activities				
Cash Flows from Financing Activities				

2 Statement of cash flows prepared

Meridian Corporation		
Statement of Cash Flows		
For the Year Ended December 31, 19x2		

1 Statement of cash flows prepared

Adams Print Gallery, Inc.		
Statement of Cash Flows		
For the Year Ended December 31, 19x2		

Computations:

1 *(concluded)*

Computations (continued)

2 *Cash problem explained*

Exercise 19-1 Effect of Alternative Accounting Methods

1 Net income determined under FIFO

2 Net income determined under LIFO

3 Method identified

4 Choice of LIFO evaluated with respect to consistency convention

5 Full-disclosure requirements assessed

Exercise 19-2 Effect of Alternative Accounting Methods

a.	
b.	
c.	
d.	

Exercise 19-3 Horizontal Analysis

			Increase or (Decrease)	
Herrera Company				
Comparative Balance Sheets				
December 31, 19x2 and 19x1				
	19x2	19x1	Amount	Percentage

Exercise 19-3 (continued)

Comment:

Exercise 19-4 Trend Analysis

	19x5	19x4	19x3	19x2	19x1
Sales					
Cost of Goods Sold					
General and Administrative					
Expenses					
Operating Income					
Comment:					

Exercise 19-5 Vertical Analysis

Herrera Company		
Common-Size Income Statements		
For the Years Ended December 31, 19x2 and 19x1		
	19x2	19x1

Comment:

Exercise 19-6 Liquidity Analysis

		19x2						19x1					
Current ratio													
Quick ratio													
Receivable turnover													
Average days' sales uncollected													
Inventory turnover													

Exercise 19-6 (concluded)

Comment:

Exercise 19-7 Turnover Analysis

Year				Receivable Turnover							Inventory Turnover				
19x1:															
19x2:															
19x3:															
19x4:															

Exercise 19-7 (continued)

Comment:

Exercise 19-8 Profitability Analysis

	19x2										19x1		
Profit margin													
Asset turnover													
Return on assets													
Return on equity													

Exercise 19-8 (concluded)

Comment:

Exercise 19-9 Long-term Solvency and Market Test Ratios

		Company B						Company C							
Debt to equity															
Interest coverage															
Price/Earnings ratio															
Dividend yield															

Exercise 19-9 (concluded)

Exercise 19-10 Preparation of Statements from Ratios and Incomplete Data

Chang Corporation										
Income Statement										
For the Year Ended December 31, 19x1										
(in thousands of dollars)										
Sales									9 0 0 0	—
Cost of Goods Sold										
Gross Margin from Sales										
Operating Expenses										
Selling Expenses										
Administrative Expenses					1 1 7	—				
Interest Expense					8 1	—				
Income Taxes Expense					3 1 0	—				
Total Operating Expenses										
Net Income										

Exercise 19-10 (continued)

Chang Corporation											
Balance Sheet											
December 31, 19x1											
(in thousands of dollars)											
Assets											
Cash											
Accounts Receivable (net)											
Inventories											
Total Current Assets											
Property, Plant, and Equipment (net)									2 7 0 0	—
Total Assets											
Liabilities and Stockholders' Equity											
Current Liabilities											
Bonds Payable, 9% interest											
Total Liabilities											
Common Stock—$10 par value			1 5 0 0	—						
Paid-in Capital in Excess of Par Value, Common			1 3 0 0	—						
Retained Earnings			2 0 0 0	—						
Total Stockholders' Equity									4 8 0 0	—
Total Liabilities and Stockholders' Equity											

Exercise 19-10 (concluded)

Calculations:

Name _____

1. Objectives identified and explained

Ratio	Objective	Importance
Interest coverage		
Pretax return on assets		
Debt to equity		
Cash flow as a percentage of total debt		
Short-term debt as a percentage of total debt		

2 *Actions evaluated*

a.

b.

c.

d.

Part A—1 Financial ratios computed

	1983				1982	

Interest coverage

Pretax return on assets

Debt to equity

Cash flow as a percentage of total debt

Short-tem debt as a percentage of total debt

Part A—2 Bond rating discussed

Part B—1 Financial ratios computed

	1986			1985		
Interest coverage						
Pretax return on assets						
Debt to equity						
Cash flow as a percentage of total debt						
Short-term debt as a percentage of total debt						

Part B—2 Bond rating discussed

1 Alternative income statements prepared

Owen Company																					
Alternative Income Statements																					
For the Year Ended December 31, 19xx																					
Income Statement Using FIFO and Straight-Line																					

1 (continued)

Owen Company						
Alternative Income Statements						
For the Year Ended December 31, 19xx						
Income Statement Using LIFO						
and Sum-of-the-years' Digits						

2 Schedule prepared

Owen Company										
Schedule of Differences in Net Income										
For the Year Ended December 31, 19xx										

3 Inventory turnover computed and discussed

4 Return on assets computed and discussed

Problem 19A-2
Horizontal and Vertical Analysis

1 Schedules showing amount and percentage changes prepared

	Kelso Corporation					
	Comparative Income Statements					
	For the Years Ended December 31, 19x2 and 19x1					
					Increase or (Decrease)	
	19x2		19x1		Amount	Percentage
Sales	800400 —		742600 —			
Cost of Goods Sold	454100 —		396200			
Gross Margin from Sales	346300 —		346400 —			
Operating Expenses						
Selling Expenses	130100 —		104600 —			
Administrative Expenses	140300 —		115500 —			
Interest Expense	25000 —		20000 —			
Income Taxes Expense	14000 —		35000 —			
Total Operating Expenses	309400 —		275100 —			
Net Income	36900 —		71300 —			

	Kelso Corporation					
	Comparative Balance Sheets					
	December 31, 19x2 and 19x1					
					Increase or (Decrease)	
	19x2		19x1		Amount	Percentage
Assets						
Cash	31100 —		27200 —			
Accounts Receivable (net)	72500 —		42700 —			
Inventory	122600 —		107800 —			
Property, Plant, and Equipment (net)	577700 —		507500 —			
Total Assets	803900 —		685200 —			
Liabilities and Stockholders' Equity						
Accounts Payable	104700 —		72300 —			
Notes Payable	50000 —		50000 —			
Bonds Payable	200000 —		110000 —			
Common Stock	300000 —		300000 —			
Retained Earnings	149200		152900 —			
Total Liabilities and Stockholders' Equity	803900 —		685200 —			

2 Common-size income statement and balance sheet prepared

Kelso Corporation		
Common-Size Income Statements		
For the Years Ended December 31, 19x2 and 19x1		
	19x2	19x1
Sales		
Cost of Goods Sold		
Gross Margin from Sales		
Operating Expenses		
Selling Expenses		
Administrative Expenses		
Interest Expense		
Income Taxes Expense		
Total Operating Expenses		
Net Income		

Kelso Corporation		
Common-Size Balance Sheets		
December 31, 19x2 and 19x1		
	19x2	19x1
Assets		
Cash		
Accounts Receivable (net)		
Inventory		
Property, Plant, and Equipment (net)		
Total Assets		
Liabilities and Stockholders' Equity		
Accounts Payable		
Notes Payable		
Bonds Payable		
Common Stock		
Retained Earnings		
Total Liabilities and Stockholders' Equity		

3 Results in 1 and 2 explained

Problem 19A-3

Analyzing the Effects of Transactions on Ratios

Transaction	Ratio	Effect Increase	Effect Decrease	Effect None
a. Issued common stock for cash	Asset turnover			
b. Declared cash dividend	Current ratio			
c. Sold treasury stock	Return on equity			
d. Borrowed cash by issuing note payable	Debt to equity ratio			
e. Paid salary expense	Inventory turnover			
f. Purchased merchandise for cash	Current ratio			
g. Sold equipment for cash	Receivable turnover			
h. Sold merchandise on account	Quick ratio			
i. Paid current portion of long-term debt	Return on assets			
j. Gave sales discount	Profit margin			
k. Purchased marketable securities for cash	Quick ratio			
l. Declared 5% stock dividend	Current ratio			

Ratio	19x2	19x1	F or U*
1 *Liquidity analysis*			
a. current ratio			
b. quick ratio			
c. receivable turnover			
d. average days' sales uncollected			
e. inventory turnover			
2 *Profitability analysis*			
a. profit margin			

*Favorable (F) or Unfavorable (U) Change

Ratio	19x2	19x1	F or U*
2 (continued)			
b. asset turnover			
c. return on assets			
d. return on equity			
e. earnings per share			
3 Long-term solvency analysis			
a. debt to equity			

*Favorable (F) or Unfavorable (U) Change

Ratio	F or U*	19x1								19x2							
3 *(continued)*																	
b. interest coverage																	
4 *Market test analysis*																	
a. P/E ratio																	
b. dividends yield																	
c. market risk																	

*Favorable (F) or Unfavorable (U) Change

Problem 19A-5
Comprehensive Ratio Analysis of Two Companies

Ratio	Morton	Pound
1 Liquidity analysis		
a. current ratio		
b. quick ratio		
c. receivable turnover		
d. Average days' sales uncollected		

Ratio	Morton	Pound
1 (continued)		
e. inventory turnover		
2 Profitability analysis		
a. profit margin		
b. asset turnover		
c. return on assets		
d. return on equity		

Ratio	Morton	Pound
2 (continued)		
e. earnings per share		
3 Long-term solvency analysis		
a. debt to equity		
b. interest coverage		

Ratio		Morton							Pound					
4 Market test analysis														
a. P/E ratio														
b. dividends yield														
c. market risk														

5 *Comparative analysis*

Ratio Name	Morton	Pound	Company with More Favorable Ratio
1 *Liquidity analysis*			
a. current ratio			
b. quick ratio			
c. receivable turnover			
d. average days' sales uncollected			
e. inventory turnover			
2 *Profitability analysis*			
a. profit margin			
b. asset turnover			
c. return on assets			
d. return on equity			
e. earnings per share			
3 *Long-term solvency*			
a. debt to equity			
b. interest coverage			
4 *Market test analysis*			
a. price/earnings ratio			
b. dividends yield			
c. market risk			

6 Use of prior years' information

1 Earnings per share computed

	19x3	19x2	19x1

2 Bonuses discussed

Exercise 20-1 Methods of Accounting for Long-term Investments

1.	
2.	
3.	
4.	
5.	
6.	

Exercise 20-2 Long-term Investments: Lower-of-cost-or-market Method

	General Journal			
Date	Description	Post. Ref.	Debit	Credit

Exercise 20-3 Long-term Investments: Cost and Equity Methods

Exercise 20-4 Long-term Investments: Equity Method

		General Journal				
Date		Description	Post. Ref.	Debit		Credit

Exercise 20-5 Elimination Entry for a Purchase at Book Value

		General Journal			
Date		Description	Post. Ref.	Debit	Credit

Exercise 20-6 Elimination Entry and Minority Interest

		General Journal			
Date		Description	Post. Ref.	Debit	Credit

Exercise 20-7 Consolidated Balance Sheet with Goodwill

	Y and Z Companies				
	Work Sheet for Consolidated Balance Sheet				
	September 1, 19xx				
Accounts	Balance Sheet Parent Company	Balance Sheet Subsidiary Company	Eliminations Debit	Eliminations Credit	Consolidated Balance Sheet

Exercise 20-8 Analyzing the Effects of Elimination Entries

	F and G Companies				
	Work Sheet for Consolidated Balance Sheet				
	As of Acquisition Date				
Accounts	Balance Sheet Parent Company	Balance Sheet Subsidiary Company	Eliminations Debit	Credit	Consolidated Balance Sheet

Exercise 20-9 Preparation of Consolidated Income Statement

	Marcus Company Income Statement	Green Company Income Statement	Eliminations		Consolidated Balance Sheet
Accounts			Debit	Credit	

Marcus and Green Companies

Work Sheet for Consolidated Income Statement

For the Year Ended December 31, 19x1

Exercise 20-10 Bond Investment Transactions

		General Journal			
Date		Description	Post. Ref.	Debit	Credit

1 *Purchase entry prepared*

2 *Eliminating entry prepared*

Date	Description	Post. Ref.	Debit	Credit

General Journal

3 Consolidated balance sheet prepared

U.S. Steel Corporation
Consolidated Balance Sheet
December 31, 1981
(in millions)

4 Purchase evaluated

Name _____

		General Journal			
Date		Description	Post. Ref.	Debit	Credit

		General Journal				
Date		Description	Post. Ref.	Debit		Credit

1 Journal entries prepared

	General Journal			
Date	Description	Post. Ref.	Debit	Credit

2 Ledger account prepared

General Ledger							
Investment in Albers Corporation							
Date (Quarter)	Item	Post. Ref.	Debit	Credit	Balance Debit		Credit

Problem 20A-3

Consolidated Balance Sheet: Less than 100 Percent Ownership

	Lobos Corporation Balance Sheet	Yost Corporation Balance Sheet	Eliminations		Consolidated Balance Sheet
Accounts			Debit	Credit	

Lobos and Yost Corporations
Work Sheet for Consolidated Balance Sheet
As of Acquisition Date

Problem 20A-4

Consolidated Balance Sheet: Cost Exceeding Book Value

	Cheever Corporation Balance Sheet	Ham Corporation Balance Sheet	Eliminations		Consolidated Balance Sheet
Accounts			Debit	Credit	

Cheever and Ham Corporations

Work Sheet for Consolidated Balance Sheet

December 31, 19xx

Problem 20A-5
Bond Investment Transactions

	General Journal			
Date	Description	Post. Ref.	Debit	Credit

General Journal				
Date	Description	Post. Ref.	Debit	Credit

Financial Decision Case
San Antonio Corporation

1 Principal factors identified

2 Investment entries prepared

		General Journal			
Date		Description	Post. Ref.	Debit	Credit

2 (continued)

		General Journal				
Date		Description	Post. Ref.	Debit		Credit

3 *Adjusting entry prepared*

4 *Sale of Brownfield shares and year-end adjustment recorded*

		General Journal				
Date		Description	Post. Ref.	Debit		Credit

Exercise 21-1 Recording International Transactions: Fluctuating Exchange Rate

		General Journal			
Date		Description	Post. Ref.	Debit	Credit

Exercise 21-2 Recording International Transactions

		General Journal			
Date		Description	Post. Ref.	Debit	Credit

Exercise 21-3 Construction of an Index

Commodity	1989		1988		1987	
Wheat	3	56	3	52	3	66
Corn	3	38	2	68	2	50
Oats	1	69	1	49	1	89
Soybeans	8	19	5	69	6	04

Price index

Percentage change

Identification of index

Exercise 21-4 Application of General Price Index

1 Calculation of total 1988 land value

Item	Historical Cost	Conversions (from Table 21-4)	Restatement in terms of 1988 Dollars

2 Gain or loss explained

Exercise 21-5 Calculation of Purchasing Power Gains and Losses

	Recorded Amount	Conversion Factor	Restated Amount	Gain or (Loss)
Company J				
Company K				

Exercise 21-6 Restatement of Balance Sheet for General Price Changes

	Recorded Amount	Conversion Factor	Restated Amount
Franklin Company			
Restatement of Balance Sheet			
December 31, 19xx			

Exercise 21-7 Restatement of Income Statement

	Recorded Amount	Conversion Factor	Restated Amount
	Geneva Car Wash		
	Restatement of Income Statement		
	For the Year Ended December 31, 19x9		

1 Effects of changes in exchange rates evaluated

2 Conditions explained

Name _____

		General Journal	Post.		
Date		Description	Ref.	Debit	Credit

General Journal

Date	Description	Post. Ref.	Debit	Credit

		General Journal				
Date		Description	Post. Ref.	Debit	Credit	

Problem 21A-2
Calculation of Purchasing Power Gain or Loss

1 Purchasing power gain or loss computed

	Recorded Amount	Conversion Factor	Restated Amount	Gain or (Loss)
Kronos Corporation				
Calculation of Purchasing Power Gain or Loss				
For the Year Ended December 31, 19x4				

1 (continued)

	Kronos Corporation						
	Calculation of Purchasing Power Gain or Loss						
	For the Year Ended December 31, 19x5						
	Recorded Amount		Conversion Factor		Restated Amount		Gain or (Loss)

2 Results discussed

Problem 21A-3
Calculation of Purchasing Power Gain or Loss
and Balance Sheet Restatement

1 Purchasing power gain or loss calculated

	Carousel, Inc.			
	Calculation of Purchasing Power Gain or Loss			
	For the Year Ended December 31, 19x2			
	Recorded Amount	Conversion Factor	Restated Amount	Gain or (Loss)

2 Balance sheet restated

	Recorded Amount	Conversion Factor	Restated Amount
Carousel, Inc. Restatement of Balance Sheet December 31, 19x2			

Problem 21A-4
Restatement of Income Statement

1 Restated income statement prepared

	Recorded Amount	Conversion Factor	Restated Amount

Carousel, Inc.
Restatement of Income Statement
For the Year Ended December 31, 19x2

2 Effects of inflation discussed

1 Alternative measures of gain identified

2 Tax computed and discussed

Exercise 22-1 Definitions of Management Accounting

1 Comparison of the statements about management accounting

2 Explanation

Exercise 22-2 Cost Flow

1 Types and flow of operating costs described

2 Differences on the financial statements

Exercise 22-3 Cost Classification

1. Period costs:	
Product costs:	
2. Direct costs:	
Indirect costs:	

Exercise 22-4 Documentation

Exercise 22-5 Periodic versus Perpetual Inventory Methods

1 Periodic and perpetual methods contrasted

2 Methods preferred

	Reason
a.	
b.	
c.	
d.	
e.	
f.	
g.	
h.	
i.	
j.	
k.	
l.	
m.	
n.	
o.	

Exercise 22-6 Concept of Three Types of Inventories

Exercise 22-7 Manufacturing Cost Flow

Exercise 22-8 Cost of Materials Used

Computation of cost of materials used:	

Exercise 22-9 Computing Total Manufacturing Costs

Downey Millinery, Inc.									
Analysis of Total Manufacturing Costs									
For the Period Ended May 31, 19x1									

Exercise 22-10 Statement of Cost of Goods Manufactured

Gordon Company											
Statement of Cost of Goods Manufactured											
For the Month Ended August 31, 19x9											

Exercise 22-11 Computing Cost of Goods Sold

McCarley Distilleries, Inc.					
Income Statement					
For the Year Ended December 31, 19x1					

Exercise 22-12 Scenarios on Ethics

1 What Mac should do

2 Kim's options

Interpreting Accounting Information
Rudolph Manufacturing Company

1 Ratios computed

a. Ratios of cost of materials used, direct labor and total factory overhead costs to total manufacturing costs

	19x1		19x0	
	Amount	Ratio	Amount	Ratio

b. Ratios of gross margin from sales, total operating expenses, and net income to sales

	19x1		19x0	
	Amount	Ratio	Amount	Ratio

2 Comments on ratios

3 Other factors and ratios suggested

Problem 22A-1
Direct Costs: Cost Flow

1 Characteristics of direct and indirect materials

2 Examples of direct and indirect materials

Direct materials:
Indirect materials:

3 *Diagram of flow of materials costs*

4 Amount due computed

Problem 22A-2
Unit Cost Computation

1 Unit cost computed by department

Department F-14																	
Direct materials used																	
Direct labor																	
Factory overhead																	
Total unit cost—Dept. F-14																	
Department G-12																	
Direct materials used																	
Direct labor																	
Factory overhead																	
Total unit cost—Dept. G-12																	
Department H-15																	
Direct materials used																	
Direct labor																	
Factory overhead																	
Total unit cost—Dept. H-15																	
2 Total unit cost																	
3 Order Sb-15 analyzed																	
Selling price																	
Less cost of goods sold																	
Gross margin																	
Gross margin as a percentage of sales																	

3 (continued)

Computations and comments:

Problem 22A-3
Cost of Goods Manufactured: Three Fundamental Steps

Padgett Metallurgists, Inc.																			
Schedules for Cost of Goods Manufactured																			
For the Quarter Ended March 31, 19x9																			
1 Cost of materials used during quarter calculated																			
2 Total manufacturing costs for quarter calculated																			
3 Cost of goods manufactured during quarter calculated																			

Name _____

Bowman and Blunt Vineyards		
Statement of Cost of Goods Manufactured		
For the Year Ended October 31, 19x1		

1 Dollar usage of materials computed

Hurlburt Pharmaceuticals Corporation

Calculation of Dollar Usage of Four Types of Material

For the Month Ended April 30, 19x2

	Natural Minerals	Basic Organic Compounds	Catalysts	Suspension Agents	Total

2 *Statement of cost of goods manufactured prepared*

Hurlburt Pharmaceuticals Corporation		
Statement of Cost of Goods Manufactured		
For the Month Ended April 30, 19x2		

3 *Income statement prepared*

Hurlburt Pharmaceuticals Corporation		
Income Statement		
For the Month Ended April 30, 19x2		

1 Direct costs identified

2 Cost per patient day computed

Equipment usage	$
Doctors' care	
Special nursing care	
Regular nursing care	
Medicines	
Medical supplies	
Room rental	
Food and services	
Total cost per patient day	

3, 4 Billing per patient day computed

	Cost	3 Normal Billing	4 New Billing Approach
Equipment usage			
Doctors' care			
Special nursing care			
Regular nursing care			
Medicines			
Medical supplies			
Room rental			
Food and service			
Totals			

5 *Billing procedure recommended*

Exercise 23-1 Cost System: Industry Linkage

Manufactured Products	Costing System
a. Paint	
b. Automobiles	
c. 747 jet aircraft	
d. Bricks	
e. Large milling machines	
f. Liquid detergent	
g. Standard aluminum cylinders	
h. Special-order aluminum cylinders	
i. Nails produced from wire	
j. Television sets	
k. Wedding invitations	
l. Limited edition of lithographs	
m. Pet flea collars	
n. High-speed lathes	
o. Breakfast cereal	
p. Original evening gown	

Exercise 23-2 Concept of Absorption Costing

Exercise 23-3 Predetermined Overhead Rate Computation

1 and 2 19x0 and 19x1 Predetermined overhead rates computed

	19x0	Expected Increase	19x1
Indirect materials and supplies	9 6 2 0 0 —		
Repairs and maintenance	2 4 9 0 0 —		
Outside service contracts	3 7 3 0 0 —		
Indirect labor	8 9 1 0 0 —		
Factory supervision	4 2 9 0 0 —		
Depreciation, machinery	1 8 5 0 0 0 —		
Factory insurance	1 8 2 0 0 —		
Property taxes	6 5 0 0 —		
Heat, light, and power	1 1 7 0 0 —		
Miscellaneous factory overhead	6 0 4 5 —		
Totals	5 1 7 8 4 5 —		

Exercise 23-4 Overhead Application Rate

1 Anticipated factory overhead determined

| |
| |
| |
| |

2 Factory overhead rate computed

| |
| |
| |
| |
| |
| |
| |
| |
| |

3 Journal entry prepared

		General Journal			
Date		Description	Post. Ref.	Debit	Credit

Exercise 23-5 Disposition of Overapplied Overhead

1 Overhead applied to operations computed

2 Overapplied overhead computed

3 Journal entry prepared

	General Journal				
Date	Description	Post. Ref.		Debit	Credit

Exercise 23-6 Disposition of Underapplied Overhead

Journal entry prepared

		General Journal			
Date		Description	Post. Ref.	Debit	Credit

Supporting computations:

Account	Balance	Percent of Total	Underapplied Overhead	Amount Charged to Account

Exercise 23-7 Job Order Cost Flow

Exercise 23-7 (concluded)

Diagram:

Exercise 23-8

1 Journal entries prepared

Date	Description	Post. Ref.	Debit	Credit
	General Journal			

2 Ending balance computed

Work in Process Inventory Control Account:	

Exercise 23-9 Unit Cost Computation

1 Total cost of each job computed

	Job A-16	Job A-20	Job B-14	Totals
Webster Corporation				
Special Cost Analysis				
JOB ORDER COST CARDS				
Direct Materials:				
Fabric Q	10840 —	12980 —	17660 —	
Fabric Z	11400 —	12200 —	13440 —	
Fabric YB	5260 —	6920 —	10900 —	
Total				
Direct Labor:				
Seamstress Labor	8900 —	10400 —	16200 —	
Layout Labor	6450 —	7425 —	9210 —	
Packaging Labor	3950 —	4875 —	6090 —	
Total				
Factory Overhead:				
Total Cost				

2 Unit cost of each job computed

Exercise 23-10 Computation of Unit Cost

	Total Costs of Order A62
Raw materials costs:	
Cedar wood	8 9 0 8 —
Pine wood	6 1 2 0 —
Hardware	1 7 3 4 —
Assembly supplies	4 2 5 —
Total materials costs	
Direct labor costs:	
Sawing department	2 7 7 1 —
Shaping department	3 1 9 6 —
Finishing department	2 1 9 3 —
Assembly department	2 9 9 2 —
Total labor costs	
Factory overhead applied	
Sawing department	
Shaping department	
Finishing department	
Assembly department	
Total factory overhead costs	
Total cost of order	
Unit cost:	

1 Advantages and disadvantages of each company's approach

2 Company taking the most cost-effective approach and reason

3 Importance of an accurate overhead rate

1 *Predetermined overhead rate computed*

Crowley Cosmetics Company
Overhead Rate Computation Schedule
For the Year Ended December 31, 19x2

Overhead Cost Items	19x0	19x1	Amount of Increase	Percentage of Change	Projection for 19x2
Indirect labor	18100 —	23530 —			
Employee benefits	22000 —	28600 —			
Manufacturing supervision	16800 —	18480 —			
Utilities	10350 —	14490 —			
Factory insurance	6500 —	7800 —			
Janitorial services	11000 —	12100 —			
Depreciation, factory and machinery	17750 —	21300 —			
Miscellaneous	5750 —	7475 —			
Total overhead	108250 —	133775 —			

Predetermined overhead rate for 19x2:

2 *Amount of applied overhead determined*

Job Order No.	Machine Hours	Predetermined Overhead Rate	Overhead Applied
2214	12,300		
2215	14,200		
2216	9,800		
2217	13,600		
2218	11,300		
2219	8,100		
Totals			

3 *Journal entry prepared*

		General Journal			
Date		Description	Post. Ref.	Debit	Credit

Problem 23A-2
Job Order Costing: Journal Entry Analysis and T Accounts

1 Journal entries prepared

		General Journal			
Date		Description	Post. Ref.	Debit	Credit

1 (continued)

	General Journal				
Date	Description	Post. Ref.	Debit	Credit	

1 (continued)

		General Journal				
Date		Description	Post. Ref.	Debit		Credit

2 Entries posted to T accounts

Materials Inventory Control

Work In Process Inventory Control

Finished Goods Inventory Control

Factory Overhead Control

Factory Overhead Applied

Factory Payroll

2 (concluded)

Cost of Goods Sold	Sales

Accounts Payable	Cash

Accounts Receivable	Prepaid Insurance

1

Property Taxes Payable	Accumulated Depreciation, Machinery

3 Under- or overapplied overhead computed

(a)   (f)

(b)   (g)

(c)   (h)

(d)   (i)

(e)   (j)

Computations:

Computations (concluded)

Problem 23A-4
Job Order Cost Flow

1 September transactions reconstructed

Materials Inventory Control

Finished Goods Inventory Control

Work In Process Inventory Control

Factory Overhead Applied

2 Cost of units completed calculated

			Direct	Factory	
Job No.		Materials	Labor	Overhead	Total

Granger House
Cost of Ending Work in Process Inventory
September 30, 19x9

3 Total cost of units sold

4 *Ending inventory balances computed*

5 *Unit cost computed*

Job 24-A:

Job 24-C:

1 Journal entries prepared

		General Journal				
Date		Description	Post. Ref.	Debit	Credit	

1 *(continued)*

Date	Description	Post. Ref.	Debit	Credit
	General Journal			

1 (continued)

		General Journal			
Date		Description	Post. Ref.	Debit	Credit

1 (continued)

		General Journal				
Date		Description	Post. Ref.	Debit		Credit

2 Entries posted to T accounts

Materials Inventory Control

Mixing Fluid — Subsidiary

MX Powder — Subsidiary

Operating Supplies — Subsidiary

2 *(continued)*

Work In Process Inventory Control

Job 16-A — Subsidiary

Job 18-A — Subsidiary

Job 20-A — Subsidiary

Finished Goods Inventory Control

Product 16 — Subsidiary

Product 18 — Subsidiary

Product 20 — Subsidiary

2 (concluded)

Factory Overhead Applied	Factory Overhead Control

Cost of Goods Sold	Factory Payroll

Operating Supplies — Subsidiary (O/H)	Factory Rent — Subsidiary (O/H)

Heat, Light & Power — Subsidiary (O/H)	Repairs and Maintenance — Subsidiary (O/H)

Outside Contractual Services — Subsidiary (O/H)	Indirect Labor — Subsidiary (O/H)

Factory Property Taxes — Subsidiary (O/H)	Depreciation Expense, Machinery — Subsidiary (O/H)

3 *Accuracy of inventory control account balances checked*

Materials Inventory Control:								
Work in Process Inventory Control:								
Finished Goods Inventory Control:								

1 *Unit costs computed*

Job Order K-1

Job Order K-2

Job Order K-4

Job Order K-6

2 *Current balances determined*

Materials Inventory	Finished Goods Inventory

Work In Process Inventory	Cost of Goods Sold

3 *Recommendations outlined*

Copyright © 1990 by Houghton Mifflin Company

Exercise 24-1 Multiple Work in Process Inventory Accounts

Exercise 24-2 Product Flow Diagram

Diagram prepared

Exercise 24-3 Equivalent Units: No Beginning Inventories

	Units to Be Accounted For	Equivalent Units	
		Materials Costs	Conversion Costs
Strefeler Stone Company			
Schedule of Equivalent Production			
For the Year Ended December 31, 19x1			
Units — Stage of Completion			

Exercise 24-4 Equivalent Units: Beginning Inventories

Peggy Enterprises			
Schedule of Equivalent Production			
For the Year Ended December 31, 19x9			
Units—Stage of Completion	Units to Be Accounted For	Equivalent Units Materials Costs	Conversion Costs

Exercise 24-5 Equivalent Units: Beginning Inventories

	Units to Be Accounted For	Equivalent Units	
		Materials	Conversion
Units — Stage of Completion		Costs	Costs

The Lucas Company

Schedule of Equivalent Production

For the Month Ended January 31, 19x0

Exercise 24-6 Work in Process Inventory Accounts: Total Unit Cost

| Dept. | Materials Costs | | | | Conversion Costs | | | | Total |
	Dollars	Equivalent Units	Unit Cost		Dollars	Equivalent Units	Unit Cost		Unit Cost
A	25000—	2000			34113—	2055			
B	23423—	1985			26130—	2010			
C	48204—	2060			20972—	2140			
D	—|—	—|—			22086—	2045			
E	—|—	—|—			15171—	1945			
Totals									

Exercise 24-7 Unit Cost Determination

	Total Costs			Equivalent Unit Costs	
	Costs from Beginning Inventory	Costs from Current Period	Total Costs to Be Accounted For	Equivalent Units	Cost per Equivalent Unit

Guide Kitchenwares, Inc.
Unit Cost Analysis Schedule
For the Month Ended July 31, 19x1

Exercise 24-8 Cost Summary Schedule

	Cost of Goods Transferred to Finished Goods Inventory	Cost of Ending Work in Process Inventory
Svensson Danish Bakery		
Cost Summary Schedule		
For the Month Ending August 31, 19x2		

Check of computations:		

Exercise 24-9 Cost Transfer: Journal Entry Required

1 Journal entry prepared

		General Journal			
Date		Description	Post. Ref.	Debit	Credit

2 Schedule reconstructed

		La Cava Paste Company	
		Schedule of Equivalent Production	
		For the Year Ended July 31, 19x9	
	Units to Be Accounted For	Equivalent Units	
Units—Stage of Completion		Materials Costs	Conversion Costs

Name _____

1 Effects of a cost-charging error pointed out

2 Unit cost analysis schedule revised

	Total Cost Analysis			Equivalent Unit Costs	
	Costs from Beginning Inventory	Costs from Current Period	Total Costs to Be Accounted For	Equivalent Units	Cost per Equivalent Unit

3 Minimum selling price per tire computed

4 Ways for preventing errors suggested

Problem 24A-1
Process Costing: No Beginning Inventories

1a Schedule of equivalent production prepared for June

Solinko Chewing Gum Company			
Blending Department			
Process Cost Analysis			
For the Month Ended June 30, 19x9			
Units — Stage of Completion	Units to Be Accounted For	Equivalent Units Materials Costs	Equivalent Units Conversion Costs

1b Unit cost analysis schedule

	Total Costs			Equivalent Unit Costs	
	Costs from Beginning Inventory	Costs from Current Period	Total Costs to Be Accounted For	Divided by Equivalent Units	Cost per Equivalent Unit

1c Cost summary schedule

	Cost of Goods Transferred to Forming and Packing Department	Cost of Ending Work in Process Inventory

Check of computations:		

2 Journal entry prepared

			General Journal		
Date	Description	Post. Ref.	Debit	Credit	

Problem 24A-2
Process Costing: With Beginning Inventories

1a Schedule of equivalent production prepared

O'Hara Food Products, Inc.			
Process Cost Analysis			
For the Month Ended February 28, 19x2			
	Units to Be	Equivalent Units	
	Accounted	Materials	Conversion
Units — Stage of Completion	For	Costs	Costs

1b Unit cost analysis schedule prepared

	Total Costs			Equivalent Unit Costs	
	Costs from	Costs from	Total Costs	Divided by	Cost per
	Beginning	Current	to Be	Equivalent	Equivalent
	Inventory	Period	Accounted For	Units	Unit

1c Cost summary schedule prepared

	Cost of Goods Transferred to Finished Goods Inventory	Cost of Ending Work in Process Inventory

Check of computations:		

2 Journal entry prepared

General Journal

Date	Description	Post. Ref.	Debit	Credit

Problem 24A-3
Process Costing: With Beginning Inventories

1a Schedule of equivalent production prepared

	Units to Be Accounted For	Equivalent Units	
		Materials Costs	Conversion Costs
Units — Stage of Completion			

Mohamad Bottling Company
Mixing Department
Process Cost Analysis
For the Month Ended August 31, 19x0

1b Unit cost analysis schedule prepared

	Total Costs			Equivalent Unit Costs	
	Costs from Beginning Inventory	Costs from Current Period	Total Costs to Be Accounted For	Divided by Equivalent Units	Cost per Equivalent Unit

1c Cost summary schedule prepared

	Cost of Goods Transferred to Bottling Department	Cost of Ending Work in Process Inventory

Check of computations:		

2 Journal entry prepared

		General Journal			
Date		Description	Post. Ref.	Debit	Credit

Problem 24A-4
Process Costing: One Process/Two Time Periods

1a Schedule of equivalent production prepared

Units — Stage of Completion	Units to Be Accounted For	Equivalent Units Materials Costs	Equivalent Units Conversion Costs
	Morlan Natural Products Company		
	Process Cost Analysis		
	For the Month Ended April 30, 19x1		

1b Unit cost analysis schedule prepared

	Total Costs			Equivalent Unit Costs	
	Costs from Beginning Inventory	Costs from Current Period	Total Costs to Be Accounted For	Divided by Equivalent Units	Cost per Equivalent Unit

1c Cost summary schedule prepared

	Cost of Goods Transferred to Finished Goods Inventory	Cost of Ending Work in Process Inventory

Check of computations:		

2 Journal entry prepared

General Journal				
Date	Description	Post. Ref.	Debit	Credit

3a Schedule of equivalent production prepared

Units — Stage of Completion	Units to Be Accounted For	Equivalent Units Materials Costs	Equivalent Units Conversion Costs
Morlan Natural Products Company			
Process Cost Analysis			
For the Month Ended May 31, 19x1			

3b Unit cost analysis schedule prepared

	Total Costs — Costs from Beginning Inventory	Total Costs — Costs from Current Period	Total Costs — Total Costs to Be Accounted For	Equivalent Unit Costs — Divided by Equivalent Units	Equivalent Unit Costs — Cost per Equivalent Unit

3c Cost summary schedule prepared

	Cost of Goods Transferred to Finished Goods Inventory	Cost of Ending Work in Process Inventory

Check of computations:		

3d Journal entry prepared

		General Journal			
Date		Description	Post. Ref.	Debit	Credit

A unit analysis may help in the solution to this problem

	April		May	

1a Schedule of equivalent production prepared

	Units to Be Accounted For	Equivalent Units	
		Materials Costs	Conversion Costs
Units — Stage of Completion			

Culley/Grove Foods, Inc.
Mixing Department
Process Cost Analysis
For the Month Ended January 31, 19xx

1b Unit cost analysis schedule prepared

	Total Costs			Equivalent Unit Costs	
	Costs from Beginning Inventory	Costs from Current Period	Total Costs to Be Accounted For	Divided by Equivalent Units	Cost per Equivalent Unit

1c Cost summary schedule prepared

	Cost of Goods Transferred to Cooking Department	Cost of Ending Work in Process Inventory

Check of computations:		

2 Journal entry prepared

	General Journal			
Date	Description	Post. Ref.	Debit	Credit

3a Schedule of equivalent production prepared

	Units to Be Accounted For	Equivalent Units	
		Transferred-In Costs	Conversion Costs
Units — Stage of Completion			

Culley/Grove Foods, Inc.
Cooking Department
Process Cost Analysis
For the Month Ended January 31, 19xx

3b Unit cost analysis schedule prepared

	Total Costs			Equivalent Unit Costs	
	Costs from Beginning Inventory	Costs from Current Period	Total Costs to Be Accounted For	Divided by Equivalent Units	Cost per Equivalent Unit

3c Cost summary schedule prepared

	Cost of Goods Transferred to Canning Department	Cost of Ending Work in Process Inventory

Check of computations:		

4 Journal entry prepared

	General Journal			
Date	Description	Post. Ref.	Debit	Credit

A unit analysis may help in the solution to this problem

	Mixing Dept.	Cooking Dept.

Management Decision Case
CT & H Cola, Inc.

1 Factors to consider in setting a selling price

2a Total production cost per unit computed

	Units to Be Accounted For	Equivalent Units		
Units — Stage of Completion		Materials Cost	Conversion Costs	Bottle Costs

2a (continued) Unit cost analysis schedule

| | Total Costs | | | Equivalent Unit Costs | |
	Costs from Beginning Inventory	Costs from Current Period	Total Costs to Be Accounted For	Divided by Equivalent Units	Cost per Equivalent Unit

Name

2b Total cost per unit computed

3 Expected total cost per unit in 19x2 computed

4 Unit selling price range recommended

Exercise 25-1 Identification of Variable and Fixed Costs

Costs	Identification as variable or fixed cost
1. Packing materials	
2. Real estate taxes	
3. Gasoline for delivery truck	
4. Property insurance	
5. Depreciation expense of buildings	
6. Supplies	
7. Indirect materials used	
8. Bottles used in the sale of liquids	
9. License fees for company cars	
10. Wiring used in radios	
11. Machine helper's wages	
12. Wood used in bookcases	
13. City operating license	
14. Employer's share of social security	
15. Machine operators' wages	
16. Outside inspection cost	

Exercise 25-2 Semivariable Costs/High-low Method

1 Variable power cost per machine hour computed

2 Monthly fixed power cost computed

3 Total variable and fixed costs for six months computed

Exercise 25-3 Breakeven Analysis

1 Breakeven point in sales units computed

2 Breakeven point in sales dollars computed

3 New breakeven point in units computed

Exercise 25-3 (continued)

4 Breakeven graph prepared—data

Units	Fixed Cost	Variable Cost	Total Cost	Total Sales

Name _____

Exercise 25-3 (concluded)

Graph prepared

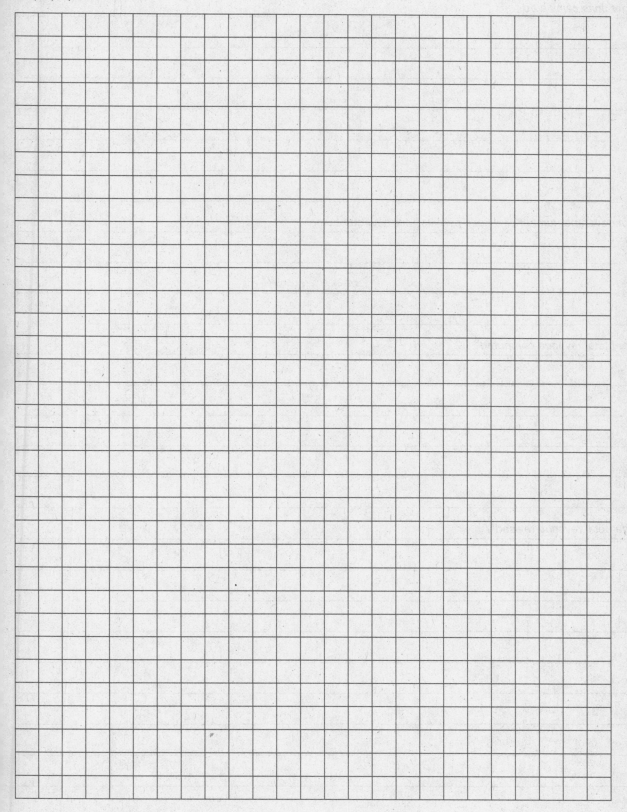

Exercise 25-4 Profit Planning

1 Target units calculated

2 Target average number of rentals per year per auto computed

3 Target total revenue computed

4 Target total revenue revised

Exercise 25-5 Contribution Margin/Profit Planning

1 Target units calculated

2 Target units revised based on new operating data

3 Additional units needed to earn higher profit

Proof:

Exercise 25-6 Cost Allocation Basis

1 Direct and indirect costs identified

2 Cost allocation basis for indirect cost and explanation

Exercise 25-7 Cost Allocation—Direct versus Indirect

Cost	Cost Objective		
	Division	Department	Product
Direct labor			
Departmental supplies			
Division head's salary			
President's salary			
Department manager's salary			
Direct materials			
Fire insurance on specific machine			
Property tax, division plant			
Department repairs and maintenance			

Exercise 25-8 Service Department Cost Allocation

Department	Minutes Used	Percent of Total	Cost to Be Allocated	Computer Cost Assigned
A	6,200			
B	8,400			
C	8,920			
D	4,160			
E	2,080			
F	10,240			
Totals				

Exercise 25-9 Joint Cost Allocation — Physical Volume Method

Product	Total Liters	Allocation Ratio	Total Joint Costs	Joint Cost Allocation

Exercise 25-10 Joint Cost Allocation—Relative Sales Value Method

Product	Liters Produced	Selling Price	Relative Sales Value at Split-off	Allocation Ratio	Total Joint Costs	Joint Cost Allocation
Grade A pulp						
Grade B pulp						
Totals						

Total joint costs computed:

Exercise 25-11 Responsibility Accounting/Organizational Structure

1 Organization chart designed

Exercise 25-11 (concluded)

2 Costs for which managers are responsible

Position	Selected Controllable Costs
Sales manager	
President	
Warehouse manager	
Cashier	
Controller	
Production supervisor	
Vice President, Sales	
Purchasing agent	
Internal auditor	
Supervisor, repairs and maintenance	
Vice president, manufacturing	
Marketing manager	
Engineering research manager	
Personnel manager	
Treasurer	
Vice president, administration	

1 Costs that should not be included in performance report

| |
| |

2 Performance report revised

	Florida Produce Company		
	Performance Report		
	Packing and Storage Department		
	For the Month Ended May 31, 19x1		
Amount Budgeted	Cost Item	Actual Amount	Over (Under) Budget

3 How should Ms. Guard respond?

Problem 25A-1
Breakeven Analysis

1 *Breakeven units computed*

2 *Breakeven dollars computed*

3 Breakeven units revised based on higher fixed costs

4 Breakeven units revised based on new operating data

1a Breakeven units computed

1b Target units computed

2   Breakeven units revised based on new operating data

3 *Selling price determined*

4 *Increased advertising costs determined*

Problem 25A-3
Allocation Process: Cost—Base Relationship

1 Allocation base selected

Type of Cost	Allocation Base
1. Cost of corporate computer center	
Discussion:	
2. Depreciation of division factory buildings	
Discussion:	
3. Tool and die making costs	
Discussion:	

1 (continued)

4. Material storage costs

Discussion:

5. Repairs and maintenance department costs

Discussion:

2 Advantages and disadvantages of pooling costs

1 Respirator costs assigned

Department	Usage Hours	Cost Per Hour of Usage	Total Cost Allocation

Computations:

2 *Alternative cost allocation bases identified and compared*

1 Joint costs allocated by the physical volume method

Product	Pounds Produced	Allocation Ratio	Total Joint Costs	Joint Cost Allocation
Totals				

2 *Joint costs allocated by the relative sales value method*

Product	Pounds Produced	Unit Selling Price	Relative Sales Value at Split-off	Allocation Ratio	Total Joint Costs	Joint Cost Allocation
Totals						

3 Schedule comparing gross profit at split-off prepared

	Extra-Rich Blend				Quality Blend				Regular Blend			
	Physical Volume Method		Relative Sales Value Method		Physical Volume Method		Relative Sales Value Method		Physical Volume Method		Relative Sales Value Method	
Sales												
Cost of Sales												
Gross Margin												
Gross Margin as Percentage of Sales												

4 Profit for extra processing of Extra-Rich blend computed

Proof:

Should the company add the extra ingredient?

1 Fixed overhead cost rate computed

Fixed overhead costs:	
Fixed overhead cost rate:	
2 Fixed overhead costs allocated	

3 *Ms. Reed's performance evaluated*

Exercise 26-1 Budgeting Principles

Exercise 26-2 Budgetary Control

Exercise 26-3 Master Budget Components

Exercise 26-4 Production Budget Preparation

Stevens Specialty Door Company				
Production Budget (in units)				
For the Year Ending December 31, 19x2				
	Garage Doors			
	Production	Sales	Ending Inventory	

Exercise 26-5 Direct Materials Purchases Budget

	January	February	March	Totals
Stevens Specialty Door Company				
Materials Purchases/Usage Budget				
For the Three Months Ending March 31, 19x2				

Exercise 26-6 Factory Labor Budget

Direct labor hour requirements schedule

Sterling Metals Company

Direct Labor Budget

For the Year Ending December 31, 19x3

Product	Standard Hours Required				
	Cutting	Grinding	Polishing	Packing	Total

Exercise 26-6 (continued)

Direct labor cost budget

	Annual Budget								Monthly Budget							

Exercise 26-7 Sales Budget Preparation

Product Class	January–March		April–June		July–September		October–December		Annual Totals	

Dockweiler Manufacturing Company

Sales Budget

For the Year Ending December 31, 19x3

Exercise 26-8 Factory Overhead Budget

Fullerton Corporation				
Factory Overhead Budget				
For the Year Ending December 31, 19x1				
Cost Category	New Orleans Division	London Division	Mexico City Division	Corporate Totals
Indirect Materials				
Indirect Labor				
Factory Supervision				
Employee Benefits				
Insurance:				
Casualty				
Flood				
Liability				
Taxes:				
Property				
Other				
Depreciation, Machinery				
Depreciation, Buildings				
Repairs and Maintenance				
Supplies				
Special Tools				
Electricity				
Miscellaneous				
Totals				

Exercise 26-9 Cash Budget Preparation—Revenues

Purposes for preparing a cash budget:

Exercise 26-9 (continued)

Storevik Car Care, Inc.

Anticipated Cash Collections

For the Quarter Ending December 31, 19x1

Credit Sales	October	November	December	Totals

Exercise 26-10 Cash Budget Preparation—Expenditures

	Cabernet Corporation					
	Cash Outflow from Purchases					
	For the Quarter Ending September 30, 19x2					
		Cash Expenditures				
Date	Gross Amount	July	August	September	Total	

1 Comment on proposed budget formulation policy

2 Recommended changes in the policy

Problem 26A-1
Budget Preparation

1 Monthly cost information prepared

October:								

1 (continued)

November:								

1 (continued)

December:

2 Quarterly budget prepared

	October	November	December	Quarter Totals
Revell Enterprises, Inc.				
Production Cost Budget				
For the Quarter Ending December 31, 19x2				

1 General and administrative budget prepared

Rogne Metal Products, Inc.			
General and Administrative Expense Budget			
For the Year Ending December 31, 19x3			
	19x2	19x3	19x3
Expense	Expense	Adjustment	Expense

2 Computer service charge distribution schedule for 19x3

3 General and administrative expense allocation and total division allocations

Division	General & Administrative Expense	Rate	General & Administrative Amount	Computer Service Charge	Total Division Allocation

1 Preliminary schedules and forecasted income statement prepared

1 (continued)

Naruse Laser Products, Inc.		
Forecasted Income Statement		
June 30, 19x1		

2 Forecasted statement of financial position prepared

Naruse Laser Products, Inc.		
Forecasted Statement of Financial Position		
June 30, 19x1		

1 Cash budget prepared

	July	August	September	Totals
Produce World, Inc.				
Monthly Cash Budgets				
For the Quarter Ending September 30, 19x2				

1 (continued) Computation of cash receipts from total sales

Cash Receipts on Account

Month	Total Sales	May	June	July	August	September

2 *Loan information discussed*

| |
| |
| |
| |
| |
| |

Problem 26A-5
Cash Budget Preparation: Comprehensive

Texas Mountain Ski Resort, Inc.

Cash Budget

For the Year Ending December 31, 19x1

Item	January	February	March	April–December	Totals

Texas Mountain Ski Resort, Inc.

Cash Budget (continued)

For the Year Ending December 31, 19x1

Item	January	February	March	April–December	Totals

1 Forecasted income statement revised

	P. C. Enterprises				
	Electronics Division				
	Revised Forecasted Income Statement				
	For the Years Ending December 31, 19x1 and 19x2				
	Budget — 12/31/x1			Budget — 12/31/x2	
Account	Amount	Percent of Sales		Amount	Percent of Sales

2 *Budget director's discussion*

Exercise 27-1 Purpose of Standard Costs

Exercise 27-2 Keeping Standards Current

Exercise 27-3 Standard Unit Cost Computation

Exercise 27-4 Flexible Budget Preparation

			Karolinski Kostume Company		
			Flexible Budget Analysis		
			For the Year Ended December 31, 19x2		
Cost Item	Variable Cost per Unit		Unit Levels of Activity		
			18,000	20,000	22,000

Exercise 27-5 Management by Exception

1 Concept of management by exception described

2 Concept applied to Falsetta-Frank Instruments, Inc.

Exercise 27-6 Direct Materials Price and Quantity Variances

Direct materials price variance computed:

Direct materials quantity variance computed:

Exercise 27-7 Direct Labor Rate and Efficiency Variances

1 Direct labor rate variance computed

2 Direct labor efficiency variance computed

Exercise 27-8 Factory Overhead Variances

Controllable overhead variance:		
Overhead volume variance:		

Exercise 27-8 (continued)

Proof:

Chapter 27 Exercises (continued)

Exercise 27-9 Standard Cost Journal Entries

	General Journal			
Date	Description	Post. Ref.	Debit	Credit

442   Copyright © 1990 by Houghton Mifflin Company

Exercise 27-9 (continued)

Computations:

Exercise 27-10 Evaluating Performance Through Variances

Exercise 27-10 (continued)

Exercise 27-10 (continued)

	Cost		Variance	
	Standard	Actual	Amount	Type

Altman Health Club
Performance Report
For the Month Ended March 31, 19x1

1 Performance report revised using flexible budget

	Budget Based on 202 Unit Sales	Actual Data at 202 Unit Sales	Variance Under (Over) Budget
GINA Realtors, Inc.			
Performance Report			
For the Year Ended December 31, 19x1			

2 *Analysis of performance report*

1 Standard direct labor cost per unit computed for 19x2

2 Direct labor standards revised based on increased production

   a. Direct labor time standard

2 (continued)

b. Total standard direct labor cost

3 Direct labor standards revised for unskilled labor

1 Total standard direct materials cost computed		
2 Standard unit cost for 19x1 computed		

3 Journal entries prepared

					General Journal					
Date		Description		Post. Ref.		Debit			Credit	

Problem 27A-3
Materials and Labor Variances

1 Direct materials price and quantity variances computed

	Liquid Plastic	Additive
Total direct materials cost variances		
Direct materials price variances		

1 (continued)

	Liquid Plastic	Additive
Direct materials quantity variances		
Proof:		

2 *Direct labor rate and efficiency variances computed*

	Molding	Trimming	Packing
Total direct labor cost variance			
Direct labor rate variances			

2 (continued)

	Molding	Trimming	Packing
Direct labor efficiency variances			
Proof:			

Direct materials variances computed:

Total direct materials cost variance

1 Direct materials price variance computed

2 Direct materials quantity variance computed

2 *(continued)*

Proof:

Direct labor variances:

Total direct labor cost variance

3 *Direct labor rate variance computed*

4 *Direct labor efficiency variance computed*

Proof:

Factory overhead variances

Total factory overhead cost variance

5 Controllable overhead variance computed

6 *Overhead volume variance computed*

Proof:

1 Standard cost per gross computed

2 Journal entries prepared

	General Journal			
Date	Description	Post. Ref.	Debit	Credit

2 *(continued)*

		General Journal																				
Date		Description	Post. Ref.		Debit							Credit										

2 *(continued)*

					Post.																
Date			Description		Ref.		Debit						Credit								

2 (continued) Analysis of direct materials purchase:

Date	Item	Actual Price	Standard Price	Difference	×	Actual Quantity	=	Price Variance

Analysis of direct materials requisitions:

Date	Item	Actual Price	Standard Price	Difference	×	Actual Quantity	=	Price Variance

Analysis of direct labor rate variance:

Date	Item	Actual Price	Standard Price	Difference	×	Actual Quantity	=	Price Variance

Analysis of direct labor efficiency variances:

Date	Item	Actual Price	Standard Price	Difference	×	Actual Quantity	=	Price Variance

3 *Controllable overhead and overhead volume variances computed*

Controllable variance:		
Overhead volume variance:		

4 *Entry to dispose of factory overhead accounts and record overhead variances prepared*

5 *Variance account balances closed to cost of goods sold*

		General Journal				
Date		Description	Post. Ref.		Debit	Credit

1 Performance report revised

Taube Aquatic Corporation — Face Wear Department					
Performance Report — Cost Variance Analysis					
For the Month Ended April 30, 19x2					
	Costs				Variances	
Supervisor: Jo Ann Wolfe	Standard		Actual		Amount	Type

2 *Supervisors' performance evaluated*

3 *Corrective action recommended*

Exercise 28-1 Relevant Costs and Revenues

1 Relevant costs and revenues identified

2 Most profitable alternative determined

Exercise 28-2 Relevant Data and Incremental Analysis

1 Relevant data

2 Analysis prepared

Bebee Industries Incremental Analysis			
	Model A	Model B	Difference in Favor of Model

Exercise 28-3 Variable Costing: Unit Cost Computation

1 *Unit cost determined*

2 *Inventory valuation determined*

Suny Corporation	Variable Costing	Absorption Costing
Unit Cost Analysis		

Exercise 28-4 Income Statement: Contribution Reporting Format

Brosi Products, Inc.						
Income Statement						
For the Year Ended December 31, 19x0						

Exercise 28-5 Make or Buy Decision

	Make	Buy	Difference in favor of

Mount Vernon Audio Systems, Inc.
Incremental Decision Analysis
Current Year—Annual Usage

Exercise 28-6 Special Order Decision

Unit manufacturing cost analysis

	Normal Product	Special-Order Product

Evaluation of proposed order:

Exercise 28-7 Using the Present Value Tables

a.

b.

c.

d.

e.

f.

Exercise 28-8 Capital Expenditure Decision: Accounting Rate of Return Method

Exercise 28-9 Capital Expenditure Decision: Payback Method

Exercise 28-10 Capital Expenditure Decision: Net Present-value Method

Year	Net Cash Inflows	×	Present Value Multipliers (14%) from Table B-3	=	Present Value

Decision stated:

1 Analysis and changes suggested

Coconino Federal Bank

Capital Expenditure Decision Analysis

After-Tax Net Present Value Approach

March 2, 19x1

Year	Increase in Cash Available from Operations	Total Taxes	Net Cash Increase	Present Value Multipliers	Present Value

1 (continued)

Year	From Operations	Depreciation	Taxable Income	Tax

2 Recommendation

1 *Unit costs and ending finished goods inventory computed*

	(a) Variable Costing	(b) Absorption Costing
Lilja Corporation		
Unit Costs and Ending Inventory Values		
For the Year Ended December 31, 19x2		

2 *Income statements prepared*

Lilja Corporation																
Income Statements																
For the Year Ended December 31, 19x2																
a. Contribution format based on variable costing data																
b. Conventional format based on absorption costing data																
Proof:																

1 Incremental analysis prepared

Rock Springs Refrigerator Company			
Incremental Decision Analysis			
Current Year—Annual Usage			
	Make	Buy	Difference in Favor of

1 (continued)

Decision:

2 *Unit costs computed*

1 Machine hours to produce one unit of each product computed

2 Profitability of each product determined

	Winslow Machine Tool, Inc.			
	Sales Mix Analysis			
	Contribution Reporting Format			
	Products			
	24F	37N	29T	40U

3 Decision on product lines made

Problem 28A-4
Capital Expenditure Decision: Net Present-Value Method

1 Decision on purchase of machines, using a 14% desired rate of return	
2 Decision on purchase of machine, using a 16% desired rate of return	

3 *Decision on purchase of machine, using an 8% after-tax desired rate of return*

Problem 28A-5
Capital Expenditure Decision: Comprehensive

1 Analysis prepared using before-tax information

a. Accounting rate of return method

Year	Net Cash Inflow	Less Depreciation	Net Income
		Increase in Net Income	

1a (continued)

1b Payback method

1c Net present-value method (minimum desired rate of return = 12%)

Year	Net Cash Inflows	×	Present Value Multipliers (12%) from Table B-3	=	Present Value

2a After-tax decision analysis: Accounting rate of return method

Year	Net Cash Inflow	Less Depreciation	Before-Tax Income	Less Taxes	After-Tax Income

2a (continued)

2b After-tax decision analysis: Payback method

2c Net present-value method (minimum desired rate of return = 8%)

Year	Net After-Tax Cash Inflows	×	Present Value Multipliers (8%) from Table B-3	=	Present Value

Name _____

Increase in net income after tax

Year	Annual Before-Tax Cash Flow	Depreciation	Annual Income Before Taxes	Taxes	Annual Income After Taxes

After-tax cash flow: net present-value

Year	Annual Before-Tax Cash Flow	Taxes	Annual After-Tax Cash Flow	Multiplier	Present Value

Recommendation to management

Exercise A-1 Future Value Calculations

1 Simple interest

2 Compounded semiannually

3 Compounded quarterly

4 Compounded monthly

Exercise A-2 Future Value Calculations

---

1 Single payment of $10,000 at 7% for 10 years

---

2 Ten annual payments of $1,000 at 7%

---

3 Single payment of $3,000 at 9% for 7 years

---

4 Seven annual payments of $3,000 at 9%

Exercise A-3 Present Value Calculations

1 Single payment of $12,000 at 6% for 12 years

2 Annual payments of $1,000 at 6% for 12 years

3 Single payment of $2,500 at 9% for 5 years

4 Five annual payments of $2,500 at 9%

Exercise A-4 Future Value Calculations

1 Compounded annually

2 Compounded semiannually

3 Compounded quarterly

Exercise A-5 Future Value Calculations

---

1 10% compounded annually

---

2 10% compounded semiannually

Year	Balance	×	Rate	=	Interest	Deposits

Exercise A-5 (concluded)

3 4% compounded annually

4 16% compounded quarterly

Year	Balance	×	Rate	=	Interest	Deposits

Exercise A-6 Future Value Applications

a *Required rate of return, $10,000 invested, $20,000 needed in 12 years*

b *Time required for $20,000 at 7% to accumulate to $32,000*

Exercise A-7 Working Backward from a Future Value

Exercise A-8 Present Value of a Lump-sum Contract

	Years	Rate	Factor	Present Value of $30,000
(1)				
(2)				
(3)				
(4)				

Exercise A-9 Present Value of an Annuity Contract

	Payments	Rate	Factor	Present Value of $600 Payments
(1)				
(2)				
(3)				
(4)				

Exercise A-10 Noninterest-bearing Note

Calculations:

Exercise A-10 (continued)

Journal entries prepared

	General Journal				
Date	Description	Post. Ref.	Debit		Credit
1	Purchase on Olson records and sale on Carter records				
	Olson Journal				
	Carter Journal				
2	Interest expense and interest earned at the end of				
	one year				
	Olson Journal				
	Carter Journal				
3	Interest expense and interest earned and payment of				
	note at the end of the second year				
	Olson Journal				
	Carter Journal				

Exercise A-11 Valuing an Asset for the Purpose of Making a Purchasing Decision

Exercise A-12 Determining an Advance Payment

Exercise C-1 Computation of Tax Liability

1 Single individual, taxable income of $12,500

1987:

1988:

2 Single individual, taxable income of $59,000

1987:

1988:

Exercise C-1 (concluded)

---

3 Married couple filing jointly, taxable income of $11,250

1987:

1988:

4 Married couple filing jointly, taxable income of $59,000

1987:

1988:

Exercise D-1 Basic Concepts and Funds

1.	
2.	
3.	
4.	
5.	

Exercise D-2 Recording the Budget in the General Fund

	General Journal				
Date	Description	Post. Ref.	Debit	Credit	
a.					
b.					

Journal entries prepared

	General Journal			
Date	Description	Post. Ref.	Debit	Credit

Journal entries (concluded)

		General Journal			
Date		Description	Post. Ref.	Debit	Credit

Exercise E-1 Computer-integrated Manufacturing — Definition

Explanation

Statement 1

Statement 2

Statement 3

Exercise E-2 Old versus New Manufacturing Environment

Comment:

Exercise E-2 (continued)

Plant layout suggested

Exercise E-3 Elements Supporting JIT

a.

b.

c.

d.

e.

Exercise E-3 (continued)

f.

g.

h.

i.

Exercise E-4 Cost Driver Determination

Exercise E-5 Costs and Their Cost Drivers

Separate cost pools recommended	

Exercise E-5 (concluded)

Alternative allocation bases — possible bases by activity:

Exercise E-6 Raw-in-process Inventory

Date	Description	Post. Ref.	Debit	Credit

1 Operations listed chronologically

2a Operations or process elements that would be eliminated under JIT

2b *Operations that should be automated*

2c *Operations that could be combined into operating FMS cells*

3 *Candidacy for the JIT/FMS environment evaluated*

1 Cost allocated based on direct labor hours

2 New overhead pools created

	Machine Hours	Cost of Raw Materials Used	Engineering Hours	Floor Square Footage	Totals
Indirect support labor					34190 —
Machine repairs and maintenance					3650 —
Materials delivery trucker wages					2820 —
Depreciation, materials delivery trucks					1120 —
Depreciation, building					2640 —
Depreciation, machinery					5370 —
Electrical power					2490 —
Machinery supplies and lubricants					1370 —
Engineering salaries					11880 —
Depreciation, engineering equipment					1450 —
Operating supplies, engineering					950 —
Fuel, raw materials delivery					310 —
Purchasing department costs					2260 —
Fire insurance, building					420 —
Property taxes, plant					550 —
Totals					71470 —

3 Plantwide overhead costs reallocated

	Sound Department	Casings Department	Totals

Discussion

4 Advantages and disadvantages of additional pools identified

5 Allocation bases compared

	Model X20	Model Y16	Totals

5 (concluded)

Allocation approach chosen and reason given

1 Total materials cost and total conversion cost computed

Material costs:	
Conversion costs:	

2a *Schedule of equivalent production completed*

	The Forest Company		
	Cost of Production Report		
	For the Week Ending July 30, 19x9		
	Units to Be	Equivalent Units	
	Accounted	Materials	Conversion
Units—Stage of Completion	For	Costs	Costs

2b Unit Cost analysis schedule completed

	Total Cost Analysis			Equivalent Unit Costs	
	Costs from Beginning Inventory	Costs from Current Period	Total Costs to Be Accounted For	Divided by Equivalent Units	Cost per Equivalent Unit

2c Cost summary schedule completed

	Cost of Goods Transferred to Finished Goods Inventory	Cost of Ending Raw-in-Process Inventory

Computation check:		

3 Journal entry prepared

Date	Description	Post. Ref.	Debit	Credit

General Journal

4 Price of Grand model discussed